A plea to think differently in the digital world

reflections on digitalization and society

By Peter Hagedoorn

Writer: Peter Hagedoorn

Editor: Rola Hulsbergen

Mail: peter@hagedoorn.org

www.hagedoorn.org

December 2020

Contents

Preface

The fluid society is a name for the digital society that humanity will grow towards in the coming years. Over the last ten years I have written many columns about the digital transformation of society, comparing the old situation with ice cubes - the nation-states - melting under digital pressure, resulting in globalization and many other effects. Hopefully a fluid society will eventually emerge in which people's work and leisure will become more virtual and international. A society in which borders are less important which will lead to more equal and fair living conditions for people worldwide.

This book contains a number of columns I have written about social developments in the fluid society. Nowadays we live in a **scrambled world**, in which everybody can live everywhere, can work digital wherever they want and yet keep in touch with their own culture. We mingle more than ever , but do not really live together. This leads to vulnerable and crumbled societies. We are also confronted with **overpopulation** and we know already that the earth is not able to provide everybody with a decent living, nor will nature be able to cope with so many people. Our way of thinking prevents the actions which are required to solve these and other global problems. As long as **"we-they" thinking** overrides "we-together" thinking, we wil not be able to solve the long term problems we have to solve to survive. The present **nation-state**, a product from classical society, seems one of the hurdles to the future. Nation states prevent people and companies from working freely together. Instead of nation-states serving their people and companies, it seems nation-states are becoming more and more an aim in themselves or tools, toys or sidebars for old men seeking power and bonuses as CEO's of nation states. How to bring back governments into a situation in which they support their people and companies, rather than using them? Into a modus of working together multilaterally to solve the huge global problems, to the benefit of all?

Governments should realize that over **50% of mankind has a smartphone**, and thus is "connected". These people absorb knowledge from internet to enrich and improve their lives. They might try to emigrate to better areas, but there is also the option to provide them with the right knowledge to improve their living in the places where they live today. It is a challenge for richer countries to prevent immigration by helping poorer countries. In the meantime the world is digitally threatened by cyber criminals, misbehaving governments, disinformation and tech giants seeking more and more profits. Society might be sucked into a **digital black hole** if we don't take measures to prevent domination by digital entities which only seek their own wellbeing. Governments should make rules for social media and internet, to keep internet free and safe for everybody.

Furthermore the labour market is heavily affected by digitalization. **Yellow vests** protests in France show the problems for those in the lower ranks, while digitalization makes some others ever richer. A new social-economic contract is required for society. It is not only the labour market that is changing. Man itself is subject of digital technologies. Will robots and algorithms take over society? Will we see half man half computer beings, connected to the internet to fill their brains? There are already experiments with

makeable humans at universities, so called cyborgs. Should we allow all these developments? Should we make happen what is possible and is that good for mankind?

In the enclosed columns I express some brief thoughts about all these subjects that are changing today's society.

The scrambled world

Published 11 November 2020:
https://hagedoorn.org/en/the-scrambled-world/

Physically living here, but mentally being somewhere else. In the digitalizing world, it is becoming ever easier to live in one place and work - digitally - in another. It is also becoming ever easier to live in a random place and stay connected to your homeland and culture. At one time it used to be necessary to learn the local language in another country - or you could not earn a living - nowadays it is quite possible to emigrate to another country and keep speaking your own language among your compatriots. In all the major cities of the world you will find people from almost every country.

What does this lead to ? We are living in a world that is becoming more and more scrambled, without a single homogeneous new "liquid" culture emerging. The liquid is, so to speak, not very well mixed yet. Whereas different cultures used to be geographically separated from each other and - given the long distances usually did little harm to each other - it is now easy to digitally conspire as a religious or extreme group worldwide and make life miserable for other groups or cultures. This partly explains the success of Islamic terrorism and the dirty tricks, lies and conspiracy rhetoric on social media and the strange attacks of "lone wolves". The scrambled world is vulnerable to evildoers. The scrambled world makes it easier to prove your supposed right by attacking innocent civilians with freely available weapons. Or by spreading fake news and thus inciting groups against each other.

Social cohesion has crumbled. One effect of the "scrambled" society with digital group formation is that social cohesion within countries and large cities is crumbling. Where people used to need each other at work, in the social environment, thus learning the language and integrating, now all kinds of groups of people live in large metropolises, completely alongside one another. Large cities are thus collapsing into tribal environments, where tribes live alone and not with each other. A similar effect can be seen between large cities and the countryside. Both environments have a totally different perception of reality, to such an extent that in the countryside one finds predominantly conservative and nationalistic thinking people, whereas the cities are progressive and cosmopolitan.

Digital transition of society. We live in the transition period from the classical world, where everyone lived in isolation in his own country and cultural background, to a digital world in which mankind will integrate and merge continuously. In which ever more services will become available on a global scale, such as those of the tech giants. In which national borders will blur in favour of global collaborative networks. Global division of labour, migration, clashes of civilizations, geopolitical turmoil, it is all part of this transition period. We are heading towards a digital world with different social structures, which at this moment we can hardly imagine.

How should we deal with this? What certainly does not work is what populists are trying to do: look back at how it used to be and present it as a desired future. Anyone who wants to move forward but keeps looking back will only bump onto something. The past was not as beautiful as it is supposed to have been and moreover, it will not return. The entanglement between thousands of sectors and organizations worldwide has already progressed too much. Closing borders is not a solution. It does not stop either digitalization or globalization, nor does it offer a solution to migratory flows. What all this will eventually lead to is an increasingly egalitarian world. That is what is particularly urgent in rich countries and within these at the bottom of the labour market.

Move with the transition. We will have to accept that humanity is in a transition period which continues and the only thing that can be done is to guide the process positively. This means that governments have to create space for the natural process of worldwide cooperation between citizens, scientists and companies. That governments must work together to tackle the major problems of our time. That governments have to adjust their laws to the international changes that are going on, reform their labour markets and learn to look beyond purely national and short-term interests.

Time for new leaders. For the time being, we irrevocably live in a scrambled world, in which we will have to deal with contradictions between people and cultures cautiously. We could at least learn that there is not one truth, but that there are different solutions to the problems we are struggling with. That it should not be "us" against "them", but "us together" working on a world where we can all live in decent conditions in a sustainable environment. In this new world there is no place for enemy thinkers like Trump. It is time for new leaders who understand the new era and guide us through this transition phase towards new social structures.

Overpopulation: the real problem

Published 5 October: https://hagedoorn.org/en/overpopulation-the-real-problem/

There are too many people. Many of us are working hard on the big problems the world is struggling with: climate problems, sustainability, biodiversity, migration problems. However, the dominant cause of all these problems is the - too often forgotten - fact that there are far too many human beings in this world. And we can tinker with all kinds of problems, but above all we must not forget that this structural problem has to be solved. Any other action, such as eating less meat, producing less CO2, is pointless, if mankind thinks this allows for more children. Mankind must set limits to the number of people with whom we inhabit the earth. The choices are roughly these: either we live on the earth with a lot of people, but in that case we all live in poverty or we will live on the earth with fewer people, in which case we will live in some kind of prosperity. We should talk about this kind of choices.

What would be the optimal number of people on earth? At this moment humanity counts almost eight billion people. These can roughly be divided into one billion relatively rich people - in Europe, North America, Japan and some other large countries - and seven billion rather poor people. The per capita consumption of the one billion rich people is roughly twenty times that of a person in a poor country. The current climate problems and other major global problems are therefore almost entirely due to the rich people of the world, given the low consumption pattern of the seven billion others.

In the year 1960, the world had three billion people. This is a reasonable number of people, who in all probability could live "eternally" on earth in prosperity and in relatively pleasant conditions, without exhausting the earth. Although what should be added is that even this, with the current level of consumption in Western countries, would be a considerable challenge. But the situation would be many times more favourable than it is now.

David Attenborough: a life on our planet. It is clear that we are in big trouble right now, as David Attenborough's latest documentary "a life on our planet" shows once again. The earth is dying, millions of animal species are in danger of extinction, large areas of land are becoming uninhabitable, millions of square kilometres of forests have been cut down, ice caps are melting rapidly, causing sea levels to rise, and so on and so forth. But the situation is still basically reversible, provided the right decisions are taken quickly and globally.

Attenborough's recommendations consist of the expectation and hope that through better education and economic development in many countries, fewer children will be born. Besides he recommends to rigorously increase solar and wind energy and to reduce the use of hydrocarbons and besides to drastically reduce meat consumption, thus making much more arable land available for vegetarian products.

Unfortunately, these efforts seem to be insufficient. All this is wise, but will it be enough, if it succeeds? As indicated, the rich of the world consume many times more than the poor. The big problem is that those poorer people are doing their utmost to rapidly increase consumption to catch up. Thanks to numerous development programs, the world's poorer people have more and more money to spend. Where until recently China was a developing country, it is now a country with the largest number of millionaires and therefore consumption is also increasing by leaps and bounds. The same goes for many other countries in Asia and Africa. While Asians, partly because of their culture but also because of poverty, used to eat little meat, they have now become big meat consumers. On the one hand, China promises to be CO2 neutral by the year 2060, but by now, with the installation of more and more coal-fired power stations, they are the largest CO2 polluter on earth.

In short: while the rich countries still have to start diminishing their consumption in many areas, consumption in many other countries is rapidly increasing.

Fewer people in all countries. It is strange and irresponsible not to put much more effort into reducing population growth. Both in rich countries, because of their current excessive consumption, and in poorer countries, because of their upcoming consumption. An argument of developing countries is that rich countries should not interfere with their policies. But that is outdated thinking. In today's world, we will have to pull out all stops in terms of policy in order to master the many and shared world problems. And collaboration, also between rich and developing countries, is the key. Moreover, without collaboration with the rich countries the developing countries would shoot themselves in the foot. The rich countries are not able to absorb the population surpluses of other countries which result in hunger and destruction of nature for countries that let population growth get out of hand. But rich countries are quite willing to make all kinds of aid available to countries that are serious about tackling this problem. The rich countries themselves should, however, not come up with plans to increase the number of their inhabitants in connection with the ageing of their populations. If they want to do so at all, they should encourage the immigration of foreigners and should not encourage their own population to have more children. The latter option is totally irresponsible. But it is also better to have fewer people in rich countries, both from the perspective of the total world population as well as from an environmental and consumption point of view.

We will have to make an extra effort. Attenborough's optimistic story that we can solve the problems within a hundred years is, although sympathetic, extremely unrealistic, given the state of contemporary politics. The world must bring more into play than Attenborough's, otherwise excellent, suggestions. Population reduction in all countries, both rich and poor, should be the number one of all environmental measures. Every mouth that consumes less is beneficial. China's one-child policy has saved us as many as 400 million Chinese. This policy has been extremely positive for the world and is worthy of the Nobel Prize. If we could keep the world under eight billion people, that would be a huge gain. That is why politicians in all countries should put this issue at the top of the agenda. Because it is simply more effective and faster than almost any other measure to save the climate or biodiversity.

Stop "we-they" thinking

Published 28 June 2020: https://hagedoorn.org/en/stop-the-we-they-thinking/

The world has been groaning under a group of authoritarian leaders such as Trump, Putin, Xi, Erdogan, Orban, Bolsanaro, with the result that no progress is being made in the transition to a more sustainable and just world. It is no coincidence that these old-school leaders are all men and democratically elected, except Xi. They represent a conservative and fearful electorate that fears change and fears that jobs may be put at risk by migrants or robots. All these leaders claim to strengthen their nation, their values and their economy in the classical way. With jobs in classic companies such as coal mines or car factories. By closing the borders. By criticism of climate scientists, globalization and internationalization. By ending international treaties and participation in international organizations, because they would not contribute to the national economy, but only cost money. By accusing other countries of attempting to steal jobs or of playing unfair competition. The thinking of these leaders is based on enemy thinking and "we-they" thinking. Everything revolves around protecting one's own country and people against foreign countries. It is the classical way of thinking that no longer fits and is no longer feasible in a world that must and will function as one whole.

It is **the tragedy of these traditionalists** that what they detest will come closer through their own actions. The demolition of classical nation-state thinking is accelerating, because the old economic theories, aimed at national enrichment and neglect of nature, are no longer tenable. Anxiously holding onto what should no longer be held onto leads to more and more protests, lawsuits and criticism from young people and intellectuals. The thinking of communist Xi and Putin and capitalist Trump and islamist Erdogan hardly differ: they all share the view that their own people and nation-state are above everything, above the interests of a wider world community, above conservation of the earth. They all run their countries as a company in competition with other countries. They all pursue world or regional hegemony with their nation-state.

But more and more people are becoming aware that **we live in one world, with one nature, one humanity**, where all people have the same rights to a reasonable and just existence, in conjunction with a healthy ecology. The consequence of this is that much more and better cooperation is required worldwide to solve the major problems of our time. The climate and ecology problems are urgent and growing. We do not want to leave a world for our children or fellow citizens in distant countries that has become uninhabitable due to increasing hurricanes or drought caused by uncontrollable temperature rises. It is impossible to maintain a prosperous West alongside a languishing Africa. And closer to home: a prosperous northern Europe versus an impoverished southern Europe.

The ever faster destruction of nature and ecology is shocking. This must be stopped. The corona pandemic, assuming this can be related to the irresponsible consumption of wild animals, gives us another warning of what can happen if we continue to destroy nature. The problem with migrants can only be solved if we do more about climate control, so that the countries of origin remain habitable. And by helping those countries to build a reasonable and perspective future for their citizens. That means that we, the rich western world must invest strongly in these countries. This is just as necessary for citizens in those countries as it is for ourselves, because hundreds of millions of migrants will have no perspective in the West either. "We-they" thinking is the impediment to doing something about the huge divides in the world. The climate crisis, migrations, the destruction of nature, the corona pandemic, make it clear to us that we must look at the world and our fellow citizens differently, more holistically.

The technology war between the governments of China and the US is a hopeless problem that will not solve anything and will only know losers. Neither the citizens of China, nor those of the US, or the rest of the world will benefit. The companies in China and the US do not want a technology war at all. Companies want to work together worldwide, because they have long known from experience that reliable and long-term international cooperation leads to the best results for themselves and their customers. So why this fight? To perpetuate the nonsense of world powers that want to become "great" and compete for the hegemony of the world? It is ego-tripping of old men who do not help the world and its citizens move forward, but rather put them in further trouble.

A major problem is that **we are stuck between old economic laws**, which stipulate that economic growth is sacred and nature is for free, versus the understanding that we will cause irreparable damage to nature and ecology if we continue as we do. We are increasingly aware of the need to change course. The question is how we do this without causing too much damage to the economy and society. When are the leaders ready to shape a more sustainable society and economy that respects nature? Economists, climatologists, anthropologists, virologists, even the financial world, warn against the dramatic consequences, including those for world economy, if politicians do not change course. Are we perhaps waiting for a female group of top leaders? Change is in the air, but there is no real turnaround yet.

We are now in the aftermath of **the corona pandemic**, which is not over yet. Which sends a new signal that humanity is on the wrong track. Looking closely it appears that destruction of nature is the underlying cause. The destruction of animal habitats, the creation of large monocultures, leads to violent counter-reactions from a plagued nature. Existing economic laws have created the fiction that mankind and its economy are separate from the nature that surrounds them. So we ask nature to supply us from seemingly infinite supplies to satisfy our excessive consumption. But the stocks are exhausted and there is only one pantry.

The corona virus has given us one more sign: **we have to change course**. The corona pandemic has led to forced rest and reflection. Society is on a hold for a moment. All around the world discussions are taking place: are we using the released billions to restart the old polluting economy or is this the unique opportunity to change course? Should we, Europe, collaborate in solving the corona pandemic with a new beginning such as a Green Deal, or will we continue in the classical wasteful way ?

Then there was **George Floyd**. The umpteenth stupid action by a white policeman in the US, resulting in the death of a black man, set the world on fire. Protests have erupted rightly everywhere against racism, against serious and long-standing injustices by government agencies against certain groups of citizens. World-wide historical statues were toppled over. May be not right, but understandable. More and more people of all colours are joining the protests. While for decades already laws have emphasized the equality of all citizens, many have not yet fully grasped or accepted this. Too many still seem to think that people who look different from themselves are inferior, have fewer rights, or should be treated differently. But in the end, perhaps because change is in the air, the anti-racism protests seem to have been taken seriously by politicians who have looked away for years. Reputable politicians now report that there is also something wrong in many government institutions. Be it the Minneapolis police services or the Dutch tax authorities.

The underlying cause of racism is "we-they" thinking. It comes down to group thinking about other groups, rather than valuing or judging people based on personal qualities. There is only one human race, but due to contrived reasoning, some groups of people do not want to accept others. It is the result of cultivating or glorifying the "own" people sentiments on the basis of so-called historical achievements, for example, the Jewish-Christian tradition. It is a remnant of colonial times, when white peoples ruled over many other peoples. It is partly the result of an ever-expanding population in urban areas, where many cultures live too close together without integration. It is motivated by fear of what is different and what can threaten one's own culture or habits.

But racism is just **another phenomenon that has to disappear under the pressure of increasing internationalization and globalization**. As more people around the world travel, collaborate and live together, the delusion that one man should be superior to another is being mercilessly dismantled. Racism is not only false nonsense, it is unsustainable and even impractical in an increasingly international world of mixed cultures. People, regardless of origin, colour, education, or location, will have to learn to work together to keep the world liveable. Racism is the very last thing we can use in this process. Some politicians are beginning to realize that racism is not only morally despicable, it is also an obstacle that must be removed to open the way for a new society that is irrevocably more international.

But it will still be a heavy task to make racism really disappear in all institutions and the minds of many in all countries in the coming years. Because "we-they" thinking is deeply rooted.

Nationalism is an extension of racism. Because "we" needed all kinds of goods, we conquered many countries, founded colonies, forcing "them", the local population or slaves, to work for us. Since "we" need raw materials or clothing, "they" must supply them cheaply or under poor conditions. Because "we" want to protect our farmers, we set import tariffs for agricultural products that "they" can also supply. Because "we" use palm oil or biomass, "they" have to sacrifice their forests. It is becoming increasingly clear that this unfair situation cannot continue. The tropical forests, the Amazon, the habitat of animals, which are destroyed by excessive western consumption, have also become a western problem and not only for those "others" who live far away. There appears to be only one world and not one for "us" and one for "them".

If it really gets through to the minds of all people that all people on earth are equal and should therefore be treated equally, this will have profound global economic and social consequences. It will not only have consequences for doing away with past injustices within countries with different population groups. It is by no means enough to apologize for past slavery that most people today cannot do anything about and do not want to have anything to do with. It is much more important that in the present active attention should be paid to improving relations between population groups and the institutions. This will also have consequences for our dealings with other countries.

Stopping "we-they" thinking means stop robbing the poorer countries of their raw materials or (palm) oil. Or the expulsion of native people from tropical forests, or the expulsion of local fishermen from fishing grounds by large companies with floating fishing factories. Or unequal treatment of products from other countries to protect "one's own people". When we think about it, our actions are swarming with "we-they" thinking and racist operations, both within our western countries and in relation to other countries.

Stopping "we-they" thinking also means that the reconstruction after **this corona pandemic should not be used primarily to strengthen the already rich countries** that have enough money, but that we should invest substantially in lagging countries and areas like Africa and South America. Fortunately, some political leaders like Macron and Merkel seem to realize this. It also means that we must use the many billions that are becoming available for post-corona pandemic recovery operations for a sustainable economic turnaround. This has been necessary for a long time, but is also justified by the need for western countries to deal more carefully with the climate and increasingly scarce raw materials, for the benefit of the many who still live in poverty.

Perhaps for decades to come there will be **only one chance to invest so many billions in the necessary sustainability and energy transition** that will benefit everyone on earth. We can not miss this opportunity. The corona pandemic has taught us that we can make much more use of digital tools to do our work and to maintain social contacts, and that this is also more efficient and sustainable. This momentum must be maintained for example, by working from home and reducing unnecessary transport. Finally, the corona pandemic could have the consequence that the necessary sustainability change will be brought about.

George Floyd's death could eventually work as **the butterfly effect in the Amazon**, which as a metaphor indicates that a minor cause, the wing beat of a butterfly, can cause a hurricane and lead to a turnaround. George Floyd's death might have the effect that it is finally and deeply understood, not only in formal laws, but also in our daily actions, that all people are equal. The consequence of this is, first of all, the elimination of racism. But the consequence of this should also be that we will realize one habitable and shared society for all people on earth and not just for "our own people". This makes us realize that national populist tendencies only create divides between people and can therefore never lead to real solutions.

Governments need to learn not to compete with each other, but given the challenges we face around the world, they need to focus on aligning laws and regulations. The principle of equality of all people has to lead to an increasingly synchronised policy between countries. It would also enhance the efficiency of public administrations and their accessibility for citizens. Equality for all people means a different way of dealing with migrants. It means more attention to the working conditions in factories that make goods for western countries. Or for the way in which many agricultural products are grown. With digital tools such as blockchain technology, chain transparency is easy to achieve and it would contribute a lot to prevent or unmask illegal or harmful production conditions.

Ultimately, the aforementioned change means **the breakthrough to another world, to the fluid society**. In which the nation-state is no more than an area where you happen to live or not live, but not one of many of states that compete with each other. Inequalities of all people must disappear step by step and everyone should be offered the same opportunities. This has not been achieved yet, not even, as George Floyd shows, in the rich western countries. But digitalization can also help us here. To accelerate the exit from the old economy, to accelerate digital collaboration worldwide, to help other people and countries digitally, to accelerate sustainability through digital working and to stop "we-they" thinking.

The Nation-State: threat to a better world?

Published 29 December 2019: https://hagedoorn.org/en/the-nation-state-threat-for-a-better-world/

Why do populists exist? Populist movements stand up for the preservation of the sovereign nation-state. These movements fear that sovereignty will flow "abroad" or to international institutes and argue for the preservation of a strong national economy, a unified population and national culture. They also criticize migration and the influx of foreign people in general. Digitalization resulting in globalization has highly influenced the course of events in societies. It has led to the growth of international tech companies and platforms which in their turn have affected many national companies and sectors. Thousands of companies are phased out due to globalization. It also leads to rigorous changes in the labour market: many traditional professions disappear in favour of tech jobs. Digitalization leads to ever increasing migration streams. So the worries of many are understandable. Digitalization and related globalization affect the existing sovereign nation-state to the very core.

Digitalization is a change agent. Ongoing digitalization and globalization will irrevocably change societies more in the coming period and have the tendency to mix people and cultures. Digitalization leads to a world that is interconnected via billions of invisible, active, digital links between people, systems and organizations. It is very important for citizens and companies alike that this international process of the hyperconnected world continues and is facilitated by political leaders. New technologies have brought humanity much good. Among other things much prosperity, better dissemination of information, more efficiency, more communication, higher quality of services. New technologies are also more friendly for the environment than old technologies. Internet access should become a fundamental human right for every citizen. Leaders like Trump or Xi cannot stop the digitalization process to go back to an authartic country. The benefits of new technologies for citizens, businesses but also society as a whole are simply too great and digitalization cannot be stopped at the border like a truck. In addition, everyone is eager to reap the benefits. But all nations struggle with the alleged disadvantages and government policies and structures have to change to cope with and absorb digital developments.

Global Platforms. One of the basic requirements for the success of both tech companies and global platforms such as Airbnb or Uber is the possibility of a global roll-out of their services. However, China and other countries with authoritarian governments fear the influences from other countries or foreign tech companies and try to stop these developments by building their own national internet infrastructures, social media and apps. Their reaction to the digitalization of society is to close their digital borders. The question is whether in the long term this can be sustained in a fluid society. The development of technologies and related sciences is in many cases too complex, too expensive, too much dependent on scarce knowledge, to be managed successfully in independency.

Why a nation-state ? To understand today's problems of the nation-state concept it is important to know the history of the nation-state. The establishment of sovereign states with a unified population, borders and - as a result - regular wars over territories or resources, is relatively new to human history. Before countries and later nation-states arose, people were small-scale farmers or nomads who moved on from place to place, normally avoiding other groups and not hampered by borders. Population growth, upcoming cities and landownership led to the situation that rulers started protecting their areas with borders and so the nation-states were born. Over the past few hundred years the densely populated "developed" nation-states, have been tending to nationalism, including feelings of superiority over other cultures, have fought other nations to protect borders and to keep foreign people and influences outside. An example of which is the two large-scale world wars in the 20th century. Today wars have become "civilised" and they are now called economic or technological wars. The political question is however: is today's concept of the sovereign, autonomous nation-state with solid borders, a nation that cultivates national values and with a unified population a solid concept that fits in with an ever more digitalized and hyperconnected world in which international cooperation and exchange on every level are more than ever required?

Own people first. It seems that the best-performing and largest nation-states, China and the US, have unambiguously chosen to continue with the sovereign nation-state concept of international independence and competition between nations. They are both in the forefront of technology because they know that whoever controls technology will become the ultimate economic winner. Both countries are also working on liberating the country from foreign influences. Own people first seems to be the main motto and not only for these nations. We see that China and US are fighting each other for power and are increasingly forcing other countries to choose for "friendship" with the one or the other. This is illustrated by - among other things - the discussion about Huawei and more recently ASML. The US will increasingly force "partner" nations to abandon Chinese technology. In the meantime China is silently creating a group of loyal "partners" who depend on Chinese technology and financial credits.

The egocentric approach of China and the US. Both the US and China have minimal interest in multilateral agreements which are so important for smaller countries. They conclude these treaties mainly to pacify or hamper other countries. For them it is much more profitable to conclude bilateral agreements with smaller countries on their own terms. Therefore neither of them wants a united and strong Europe. Strong and big nation-states lead to strong or authoritarian leadership. Big countries, big egoes. It is naive to assume that countries such as China and the US will be much concerned about the wishes or needs of small countries, take an interest in doing good for the world at large or will promote democratic behaviour. They only care about the "general good" as long as it fits in with their national interest. Neither China nor the US will abide by judgments of an International Court of Justice. Or will, against their alleged self-interest, participate in a climate agreement, the WTO, UN (United Nations) actions or whatever multilateral agreement. They simply will never allow the rules of an international organization to overrule their own national rules or policies.

Threat to small nations. Strong nations such as China, the US and to a lesser extent Russia and India are therefore increasingly becoming a threat to smaller nations or to progress on a global level. As with companies that have become too big, it would therefore be better for humanity if we could split these nations up into smaller countries. It is clear that it would be much easier to come to global understanding, multilateral cooperation and agreements. However, what is going to happen in the years to come is quite the opposite. China and the US will further cultivate their nation-state concept with their self-centred approach and will compete with each other and other nations for economic dominance.

Conflicting interests of China and US and their big companies. The result is that a controversy is growing between the policies of bigger companies and that of sovereign nation-states. Businesses flourish by international cooperation and exchange and not by competition between nations. Companies like Huawei are hampered by being linked with the Communist Party. And that applies to all companies in China. American companies want to do business with the whole world, not hampered by American sanctioning, security (Patriot Act) or trade barrier laws. Meanwhile, European companies, like ASML and NXP, are increasingly affected by the feud between China and the US.

Stuck citizens. Citizens are getting more and more stuck between two worlds. People embrace new technologies and all related possibilities like travelling and the use of social media. People are shopping around more and more - online, physically or in thoughts - in other countries and they see what might be lacking in their home country. In day-to-day reality they are sometimes confronted with all kinds of changes in numerous sectors, including the labour markets. It explains today's dilemmas of almost all political parties. The division in left and right has lost its meaning in a world where the basic struggle is between national and short term needs versus globalization, ecological problems and long term issues. And in all cases digitalization is the major change agent.

Contradictions. If we want a peaceful world contradictions should decrease, which can be facilitated by the digitalization of society including digital international cooperation. Maybe we have to partly return to the situation before the upcoming of the sovereign nation concept. Instead of protecting themselves against "others" by means of numerous national regulations, nations should just facilitate free movements of people, should stimulate companies to cooperate internationally and should synchronize their laws and regulations with other countries. Politicians should understand that the aim is not to compete as nations-state to optimize their own state, but that nation-states should primarily serve, and facilitate their people and companies to freely cooperate internationally, within commonly agreed boundaries and regulations.

The fluid nation. So we need a new nation-state concept anticipating on the further digitalization of societies in which nations should synchronize their laws and regulations in order to facilitate citizens and businesses. The concept of a fluid nation state, liberal, open to external influences and internationally connected, but besides also preserving national or regional values or habits. Fluid nations in which the big cities can function as switchboards between the international exchange of people, organizations, economies and cultures. In most big cities you can already find almost every nationality, whereas the original local cultures are preserved in small cities and remote areas.

The European project. In this respect Europe is an interesting experiment. In Europe we see that major, international questions are more and more coordinated on a European level. For example climate issues, migration, food & agriculture, international defence, cyber criminality, long term research, etc.. It is generally agreed that these questions can only be adequately solved on an international - or at least European - level. Member states and the European Commission should unravel more precisely which tasks should be allocated to the European Commission (in principal long term policies of an international nature) and which ones to the member states (in principal typically regional questions). This will save money, give clarity, motivate people for Europe, increase efficiency. What sense does it make that each European country has its own foreign affair or defence policy? And different railway or telecom systems? Different national interpretations of European laws? Or thousands of national standards instead of clear European ones? More should be done by individual member states to promote the free flow of people, services and goods. Although written down in formal European laws, most countries are obstructing these laws in practice in an attempt to protect what they consider their national interests.

Europe can show the way to modernization of nation-states. If the European Commission functions well, Europe could become an example for other regions or the entire world as to how cooperate peacefully together on major international issues, while also preserving national independence. From Brexit we can learn that European countries are already much more integrated by European regulations than most people had realized before. Europe is taking major steps in reshaping the basic concept of a modern nation-state. Accountabilities should be further defined on a national and European level. However, we should be realistic and understand that Europe has still a long way to go. In particular Eastern Europe is far from ready to accept the free flow of people or from allowing "Brussels" to take the lead on international issues. On the other hand things have gone rather well so far: Europe has been free of major wars for over 75 years now. Quite an achievement for a region that used to have wars since nation-states have existed.

Some hope ? It is hoped that despite the opposition of many nations more national regulations and laws will be replaced by global regulations and rules. Or at least - for European countries - by legislation on a European level. We should also have some hope that the younger generations, speaking better English and travelling so much more, will understand each other better than older generations. This is the hope for the future and should create a more egalitarian world, which is better for everyone. At this moment particularly large nation-states like China and the US are major stumbling blocks for global cooperation in whatever form. But technological developments are unstoppable, thus also China and the US and some other countries with authoritarian leaders unavoidably will have to change their rules under pressure of their own citizens and companies. So it may well be possible that in 2117 there will be a fluid society in which today's nation-states are differently defined and functioning. In which European or global entities govern in accordance with global rules and rulings for the benefit of every world citizen.

Everyone a smartphone

Published 12 May 2020: https://hagedoorn.org/en/everyone-a-smartphone/

Suddenly they see the world ! At the moment about 4 billion people on earth have a smartphone with an internet connection. About 3 billion of them are active on social media. What does this mean? All these 4 billion people can see how the others in the world live and work. How they live, what they think, how they make money. Most of the poor did not have a newspaper before, nor any other means of communication with the big outside world. On average, their living and thinking world did not get beyond the village where they live or beyond a communal TV. Suddenly their smartphones show them a world that they may have heard of, but have never seen with their own eyes. Suddenly information on almost all subjects is available for free and daily news in the world can be followed. Suddenly they see what they are missing, how their lives might be different, how much better things are elsewhere. And what is even more important: they can easily contact fellow countrymen who live in rich countries. What are their feelings?

What are they going to do ? What would you do ? Here are some results of some research in this area. In 2020 two hundred seventy-two million people were "migrants" (UN World Migration Report 2020). That is 3-4% of humanity. Almost double the figures of 2000: 150 million. The ages of three quarters of these are people average from thirty to forty: in short, potential workers from their countries of origin. Almost all migrants have a smartphone with an internet connection. This way they are inspired to start their journey. The smartphone is their life line with the new digital world and with the home front. The smartphone gives them information where to go and how to get there. Many try their luck in coordination with their family. The aim is to end up in one of the rich countries, find work there, and then provide the home front with money.

Everyone connected ? The number of smartphones with access to the internet varies from almost 100% in developed countries where many people already have had internet for years to approximately fifteen percent in Asia and Africa. This means that in less developed countries, hundreds of millions of connections will be added every year: one to two million a day. In the coming years, the poorest part of the world population will therefore also get smartphones with an internet connection. We can assume that in ten years time all adult people who can somehow afford it will have a smartphone with an internet connection. The world will then almost be 100% interconnected, from person to person, regardless of location.

Migration will increase. And what will the poorest people on earth do if they, like many others, can see where there is well-being and wealth? They are worse off than the 272 million people who are currently migrating. What if they become aware that there is no perspective in their country because of war, drought, floods, lack of education or health care? These people might be poor, but there is no reason to believe they are stupid. The chances are that the flows of migrants will increase considerably in the coming years. And that will certainly not get better if the rich countries get richer after the corona pandemic, whereas they fail to help the poorer countries.

Fatal dichotomy ? At this moment more than a quarter of a billion people are adrift. That could become as much as one billion in the coming decades. With all its consequences in countless places in the world where countries will try to close borders. A fatal dichotomy might arise in the world between rich countries that are increasingly taking draconian measures to protect themselves against migratory flows and poor countries that are faced with the disappearance of their only chance of perspective: the young generation. This should not happen, but it could if no action is taken.

All connected. Western countries must realize that we have entered a digital society in which everyone and everything is connected everywhere. Just like smartphones allow the poorer people to get a glimpse of how the rich on earth live, at the same time the rich can reach the poor on earth. After all, all those people with their smartphones and internet connection are digitally accessible.

Young people go to cities. The western world has to wake up quickly from its introvert attitude and not passively wait for more people to migrate. In a world with little communication it is possible that separate regions survive in isolation. But this is becoming increasingly difficult in a world where everyone is connected to everyone. Just as in richer countries the countryside is emptying in favour of ever-expanding cities, so worldwide the poorer countries will become even poorer, if the young people will leave those countries to migrate to rich countries with better perspectives.

Knowledge is the key. It is vital for both rich and poor countries to reduce these migration flows. Potential migrants must therefore be given a digital perspective, with knowledge, projects and money, to learn to build a reasonable life at their home location through digitalization, because they do not leave for their pleasure, but because of bitter necessity. It is the responsibility of governments of rich countries to provide all citizens of the world with basic information on many matters like health, education, accounting and finance, language skills, knowledge about agriculture and so on. Backed up by projects, programs and money, to convert the digitally acquired knowledge into activities to build an existence.

Develop international communication. If we are able to digitally provide people in poor countries with the information they need to help themselves to grow food, to get education and many other things, this is the best and only option to discourage potential migrants to start travelling. The digital connections also offer opportunities, depending on the right information and conditions, to temporarily attract migrants for certain activities in rich countries. But only on mutually agreed conditions and with clear information about the expectations. It may help to prevent people without perspective from ending up for years in camps in border areas. Perhaps certain migrants can work as seasonal workers in rich countries for several months. Perhaps some migrants with proven knowledge can get internships, after which they can start a business in the country of origin. Perhaps digital contracts for specific activities can be concluded with young people. And of course all this will have to be done in accordance with the governments of the countries involved. In short: much more communication needs to be established with the millions of migrants as well as their home countries, to inform them, to transfer knowledge, to try to give perspective through digital means.

One Fluid Society. One thing is certain. In the hyperconnected world, the world is becoming a digital unity. The tech giants technically connect everyone to everyone and everything. Everyone has insight into the functioning of the world elsewhere. Social media add the human component to this. The dependencies and influences on each other will continue to increase in the coming years. Step by step this fluid society will start functioning as one world. Resistance to this process is pointless, counterproductive and unwise. Governments must accept this development, look beyond "own people first" and realize that global digital connectivity will also lead to new forms of digital human connections and interactions. They should guide and facilitate this process by better cooperation. Digital connections offer new perspectives for countries, rich and poor, as well as for people, rich and poor. This requires new forms of management and governance. Ultimately for the benefit of everyone.

The Digital Black Hole

Published 21 October 2019: https://hagedoorn.org/en/the-digital-black-hole/

Governments are losing control. Society is being drawn into the digital world step by step. Digital platforms, cyber criminals, the super rich and dubious regimes increase their power in a world in which the digital economy will soon dominate the classical economy. Due to lagging legislation and national impotence, governments are losing control over digital companies, cybercrime, numerous new digital developments, the growing digital economy and, finally, society as a whole. We are in danger of ending up in a disordered society, where the - digital - right of the strongest will become the norm. Some examples will be mentioned below.

Cyber crime is totally out of control and has become a very profitable international business of around € 1200 billion in 2018. The criminal world has been totally turned upside down by the possibilities of digital technology (ransomware, phishing, etc.) and criminal platforms, so that criminals can achieve maximum results at low risks (zero chance of being caught), negligible costs and without physical victims. As an example ransomware as a Service (RaaS) can be mentioned by means of which IT systems can be held hostage. RaaS can be bought cheaply on the so called darkweb, a website for criminals, as a service for cyber criminals. Governments hardly put up a defence, in particular because this extortion uses hazy international routes. Conspiracy has never been so easy.

But the protection of **data privacy** in general is a nightmare. China, the US and other countries increase their grip on data files because of their importance for national security. Tech giants use and manipulate private data to expand their business. Regularly private data are accidentally arriving in the public domain, due to sloppy data protection of organizations or due to hackers. So nobody can be sure that his private data are not being robbed, or held hostage, or monitored by a government or accidentally published. The police mainly fight traditional thefts. But where can you go for digital accidents with your private data ?

Information is increasingly stored **in the cloud**. Governments, citizens and companies often do not know where their data are or what is happening to them. Most European companies and private persons store their data in clouds of American companies under American security jurisdiction. Not a pleasant idea.

The financial world is increasingly dominated by algorithms that partly function autonomously, which, within milliseconds, allows capital to be transported from one part of the world to another on behalf of the super-rich, criminals or financial companies. National governments have hardly any insight into international money transactions anymore.

Fake news, deep fakes and conspiracy theories directly threaten democracy. Elections have been influenced in the US. The UK has moved to a Brexit based on fake messages. Deep fake techniques allow the makers to make well-known people say whatever they want them to say. Citizens no longer know who or what to believe and are constantly manipulated by algorithms or might be drawn into conspiracy theories. Some politicians are actively using these technologies to influence their voters. There is not much we can do about this, because things are often organized on an international scale.

The **digital power** of large countries such as China and the US is unknown but very big anyway. They can effortlessly hack each other's infrastructure or other sensitive systems. That they are quite far advanced with respect to cyber warfare with each other or other countries is certain.

Artificial intelligence and robotics are rigorously and permanently changing the labour markets, by automating labour that was previously done manually. Not much thought is given to the many ethical dilemmas and social consequences of applying the many new technologies. **Software** in many large organizations or installations (Boeing 737 MAX) might suddenly turn out not to work resulting in major accidents or disruptions. It takes days, sometimes months, for the error to be discovered because software is often poorly documented and supervision hardly exists.

Increasing **digital chaos** is imminent. The world is landing into growing digital chaos as the economy continues moving to cyber space. Cyber space is a irregulated digital jungle, in which accepted rules hardly exist. Irrevocably, more and more serious digital incidents will occur in the years to come, like climate change is causing more tornadoes, draughts or flooding. As is the case with climate change, the conclusion must be that we can only manage the expanding digital problems by cross border cooperation between all countries and major tech companies. There is a need to establish some kind of global "digital agreement" to cover a great number of digital topics. As in the case of climate change, time has come for a radical change in how we manage cyber space in society: the digital risks are becoming too big and are unmanageable by individual nations.

Conclusion. If such a worldwide consultation does not succeed, human society is in danger of getting pulled into a digital black hole step by step. The super rich, criminals and corrupt regimes will continue to increase their grip on citizens, companies and society thanks to new technologies. More and more new technologies will be applied without any form of regulation or control, while ethical guidelines simply do not exist at all. Due to all digital developments, society is in danger of being held hostage in a digital black hole by groups of elusive people and by means of numerous uncontrolled technologies.

Yellow Vests

Published 5 December 2018: https://hagedoorn.org/en/yellow-vests/

Or how digitalization divides the labour market

Dichotomy. For weeks France was plagued by actions by the "yellow vests". People who organized themselves through social media and initially protested against higher petrol prices. In the meantime we saw comparable actions in other countries. What happened here?

This action is a well-known occurrence in a long series that has resulted from the transition from classical industrial society to a digital one. In this digital society highly educated people increasingly work in big cities and, moreover, thanks to technology, not location-bound, while people doing manual labour depend on others in the choice of their workplace. They are highly dependent on a car or other transport to get to places where they can do their work, while the first group can use public transport in large cities or can work from behind a computer. This dichotomy between two categories of people in society occurs all over the world and is growing due to digitalization. In the US, large groups of workers are losing their jobs when car factories close, in France entire villages are deserted. More in general, people doing manual labour in traditional companies, are in a losing position. First because manual labour is partly replaced by robots or automation. Secondly because in the digital society many traditional products are replaced by digital equivalents. Thirdly because many factories, used to making local products, are no longer needed or replaced by global companies producing for the world market. While the world is more and more becoming one marketplace, the labour markets are equalizing and otherwise heavenly shaken up due to the need of totally different products and production methods.

Understanding digitalization. Digitalization is the cause of more and more people doing manual labour being expelled from production processes, while the economy is flourishing. This is a mystery to many economists, who still expect that a growing economy will also lead to lower unemployment or higher wages. In the digital economy, however, a growing economy is partly accompanied by fewer labour options for large groups of people. In addition, the smaller group of highly educated and well-paid people will be in great demand. In fact, that process has only just started, but will irrevocably continue in the coming years as more traditional products and services are replaced by digital services.

It is about time that politicians and economists understand that worldwide a gigantic digital transformation is taking place. This digital transformation has a much greater impact on society than the disappearance of retail shops which are replaced by online webshops. The digital economy functions completely differently from the classical economy. This leads to a labour market functioning differently, with, for example many more self-employed people. There will be a greater divide between groups that do manual work and others who perform intellectual work not linked to a particular place. Also a more international labour market, considering people can work from behind their computers, with a high demand for people with IT skills.

Growing migration. Non-local international work is currently being reorganized and optimized at a rapid pace. Where in the past all kinds of companies outsourced activities to cheap labour countries, now more and more work is done from behind a computer, making it irrelevant where the employee is located. A growing group of employees doing brain work has less need to organize their work in large central offices. Work is, as it were, delivered at home. This is in sharp contrast to the work of the people who perform classical manual labour. Their work is by definition city or region bound and they are therefore much less internationally oriented. Migration also plays a major role for this group of people. After all, about 3.5% of humanity is now adrift and is looking for work in countries where they find work or the pay is better than in their home countries. This means that worldwide this labour is levelling in terms of labour costs. It is why classical manual work in many countries is threatened by digitalization and automatisation on one side and on the other side by migration of cheap labour.

The future manual labour. Consequently a dichotomy of humanity is what is currently occurring worldwide. And different working conditions are needed for both groups. The internationalization of numerous laws is important for people who perform digital brain work in order to enable them to operate internationally. And because their work is location independent, they want to live comfortably in a pleasant place. How different that is for the people who do manual labour. Their work is by definition meant to serve the elite who perform intellectual work. They will have to do their work wherever their manual labour is requested. Where the elite want to live or work, manual labour is needed, but at the same time the expensive residential areas can only be paid for by the elite. Manual workers have to travel daily by car or public transport to go to their cheaper homes on the outskirts. Meanwhile, the perspective for people who have to do manual work are dwindling. In a digitalized society manual labour will always be needed, but the number of people needed will inevitably decrease.

New solutions are required. This is the underlying cause of the protest of the Yellow Vests. Digitalization is leaving heavy marks on our society and the labour market. A dichotomy of society is taking place and will increasingly lead to two different groups of people in society with different perspectives and consequently other needs. It is about time that policymakers and economists come up with new social-economic concepts for the digital society. In France President Macron will have to prove he has understood the situation and is challenged to propose solutions.

Makeable humans

Published 9 April 2019: https://hagedoorn.org/en/makeable-persons-2/

Tinkering with humans

There has been a lot of fuss about the Chinese twins conceived in China with modified DNA with the aim of protercting these babies form HIV infection in the future. Scientist He Jiankui received the full load of criticism even from Chinese scientists.

What is the underlying moral problem? Technology is now so far advanced that in the coming years there will be countless possibilities to modify people: the make-able human. Modifying DNA or adding a chip with effects on hereditary characteristics.

Brain - computer links. We are also able to link the human brain to computers allowing people to "enrich" themselves with the intelligence or memory of computers, or to listen directly to music. Some people have built-in chips that can log in to their computers, homes or bank accounts. Experiments are done with brain-computer connections, so that you can operate a device through brain power. And of course technology helps many people with physical defects to regain a decent life: from artificial legs and arms to digital replacements of your eyes or ears. In short: a range of possibilities has unfolded to create modified people. Undoubtedly, the tech giants will also come up with consumer gadgets in this area. How should we deal with this?

Limits to manufacturability? How should you view this from the technology side? Should you develop or engineer everything that is possible or are there limits? And if so: who should set these limits? We will have to find answers to the question where, how and when certain technology can be applied. If we do "nothing", there will undoubtedly be many incidents in the coming years, as was recently shown in the case of the Chinese babies. The CRISPR-Cas technique with which DNA parts can be cut and pasted is extremely simple and can be carried out cheaply.

Making a brain link with a computer, like the cyborgs, is a bit more complex, but influencing data systems with brain power might be easy to learn.

"Improved" people? As humanity and IT specialists, we have to prepare ourselves for the path that we are taking if we are going to make "improved" or "refined" people by means of technology. The options we have range from curing sick people, which most people have no trouble with, to equipping non-sick people with extra qualities, which many people will object to. But there is a large grey area between these two options we should carefully discuss. The case of the Chinese babies is a good example. The scientist involved wanted to save the babies from a future disease through "race improvement". Is this curing a human from a possible illness, or is this racial improvement of a human? How should we cope with the many possibilities in this area that are unfolding today? More brain or memory capacity, a brain connection to the internet or computer, a physically stronger body, resistance to diseases, a longer life, a digitally smart person. What are the pitfalls to this pursuit of "Übermenschen"?

Reflection required. It is urgently required for governments, scientists, philosophers, but also the professional group of technologists, to start considering these questions. Every day technology is becoming easier and it is becoming cheaper to carry out lots of these kinds of experiments. Some rich people or scientists will take the plunge and start experimenting, perhaps with themselves, as cyborgs do. Certainly, some governments will state that they want to improve their people. Where have we heard this before? No doubt doctors will come up with proposals to make humanity resistant to certain diseases, such as HIV or malaria. Do we really want this? How should we cope with this?

International frameworks required. It would be insane to come up with different rules for each country. That is not workable and would turn out to be counterproductive. After all there is no denying that we live in one "fluid" society! The only way is a communal one but this will be a long and complex process in a world with so many contradictions. International committees should be set up to study the many different issues and provide binding advice. There are no such committees at the moment. In 2020 mankind is stuck with countless challenging and promising technologies to take people to a higher level, but is by no means able to cope with them wisely. The image that emerges is that of a toddler with a hand grenade that can joyfully pull the pin out at any moment.

Guidelines for technical staff are required. At the moment the technological man or woman who is confronted with these matters in his work has no guidelines but his own conscience. Therefore it is important that the technology community should focus more intently on the ethical side of the profession. People like the recently deceased physicist Stephen Hawking and the still very much alive entrepreneur Elon Musk have rightly pointed this out. Perhaps just as with doctors taking an oath of Hippocrates, something needs to be done so that technical professionals commit themselves to adhering to certain professional rules. It is certain that technology not only has many good but also many dangerous aspects. The ethical component has been too long and badly neglected but requires the full attention of professionals as well as society as a whole.